THE HARLEM RENAISSANCE

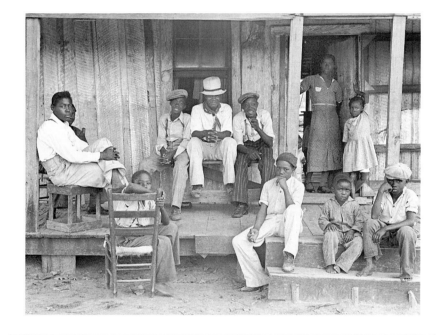

By Stuart Kallen

ABDO
& Daughters

Visit us at
www.abdopub.com

Published by ABDO Publishing Company, 4940 Viking Drive, Edina, MN 55435.
Copyright © 2001 by Abdo Consulting Group, Inc. International copyrights reserved in all countries. No part of this book may be reproduced in any form without written permission from the publisher.

Printed in the United States.

Edited by: Paul Joseph
Graphic Design: City Desktop Productions

Cover Photos:Corbis
Interior Photos: Corbis

Library of Congress Cataloging-in-Publication Data

Kallen, Stuart A., 1955-
     The Harlem Renaissance / Stuart Kallen
          p. cm. -- (Black History)
     Includes index.
     ISBN 1-57765-468-4
     1. Afro-Americans--Intellectual life--20th century--Juvenile
literature. 2. Harlem Renaissance--Juvenile literature 3. Afro-
Americans--History--1877-1964--Juvenile literature. 4.
Afro-American arts--History--20th century--Juvenile literature. 5.
Afro-American intellectuals--Biography--Juvenile literature. 6.
Harlem (New York, N.Y.)--Intellectual life--Juvenile literature. 7.
New York (N.Y.)--Intellectual life--Juvenile literature. [1. Harlem
Renaissance. 2. Afro-Americans--Biography. 3. Afro-American
arts. 4. Arts, Modern--20th century.] I. Title.

E185.6 .K25 2001
973'.0496073--dc21   00-056887

CONTENTS

Testimony to the richness and longevity of African-American musical talent from the 1930s, the large cast of the 1943 film *Stormy Weather* included the venerable Bill "Bojangles" Robinson, Lena Horne, and Cab Calloway.

CHAPTER 1

THE CENTURY OF SLAVERY ENDS

The Struggle Continues

By 1890, almost eight million black people lived in the United States. The majority of these blacks were rural workers in the South. Their main skills were farming and growing cotton. But years of cotton

Children and adults gathered on the porch of a home in a sharecropper community.

5

growing had worn out the South's soil. Growing cotton was less profitable than it had once been. Many free black people could not afford land and supplies. They were forced to work for their former owners. These owners lent blacks seeds for crops and let them live on their land in one-room cabins. When the crops were harvested, the black tenants were supposed to receive a share of the profits. This practice was called sharecropping. But dishonest bookkeeping and overcharging prevented the sharecroppers from earning much money. In practice, this system was not much better than slavery.

The Ku Klux Klan in a ceremony of cross burning.

Cotton prices reached an all-time low after a depression during the 1870s. Agricultural workers, both white and black, had a "hard row to hoe."

The Ku Klux Klan had succeeded in terrorizing blacks to keep them from voting. Between 1890 and 1990, over 1,300 mob murders against blacks were reported in the South. In 1900 alone, 114 black people were hung, burned, or shot. Life was not much better in the North. White mobs killed blacks and burned their homes and businesses. This terror kept blacks away from voting. In 1901, the last black U.S. congressman, George White, left office. Most federal officials simply ignored racist behavior. The pattern was the same in state and local governments.

Industry and Black People

After the Civil War, wealthy northerners headed South and bought up much of the shattered economy. The South was rich in the supplies needed for industry: water power, iron, coal, and oil. Factories and railroads were built using underpaid black labor. When the factories opened, the new jobs went to white workers. When blacks were hired in the factories, it was for heavy labor at the lowest wage.

Many skilled black workers from the Civil War days—brickmasons, printers, painters, carpenters, and mechanics—saw their jobs given to white workers. Often, the only jobs open to blacks were road building, sewer digging, street cleaning, rock quarrying, furnace stoking, and mining. One-third of all black workers were female maids, cleaners, cooks, and laundresses. These were the lowest-paying jobs in America. Most of the unions that fought to protect white workers did not allow black members, so some black workers formed their own unions.

The worst exploitation of black workers was the "convict lease system" or chain gang. If a black man committed a petty crime, like stealing food, he was given a long sentence on the chain gang. Once on the chain gang, the convict was dressed in black-and-white-striped clothes and chained to other prisoners at the ankle. The

prisoners were forced to build roads, dig ditches, and farm crops. Chain gangs were rented out to private industries. The state earned money while the convicts did backbreaking labor in the hot sun for no pay.

Chain gang workers

CHAPTER 2

VOICES OF HOPE

The early 1900s were difficult years for many black people, but voices of hope came from the darkness. Gifted blacks joined together to help their people rise above prejudice. From the ashes of hatred, cries of protest rose in unison.

Here are a few profiles of great black leaders from the early 1900s.

W.E.B. Du Bois (1868–1963)

Author, Civil Rights Leader

William Edward Burghardt Du Bois is considered the greatest black leader of the early twentieth century. He was a gifted scholar, writer, and advocate for human rights.

W.E.B. Du Bois was born in Great Barrington, Massachusetts. His parents were of African, French, and Dutch ancestry. Du Bois was a gifted student. He graduated from high school at 15 and entered Fisk University in Nashville, Tennessee. During the summers, Du Bois taught poor black children in dirt-floored, log-cabin schools. After graduating, he became the first black person to earn a Ph.D.

W.E.B. Du Bois

from Harvard. Afterwards, Du Bois wrote his first book, *The Suppression of the Slave Trade*. Soon he became a professor of Latin, German, Greek, and English at the University of Pennsylvania. Later he taught history, economics, and languages.

While teaching, Du Bois joined several groups that demanded equal rights for black people all over the world. Beginning in 1900, he organized a series of conferences. At these conferences, he promoted independence for countries in Africa that were under European rule. Du Bois spent over 50 years fighting for the freedom of Africans.

In 1903, Du Bois published *The Souls of Black Folks*, a book about the problems that black Americans faced in everyday life. It became a best seller. In 1905, Du Bois gathered black leaders and educators at Niagara Falls, New York. This group was known as the Niagara Movement. It became the forerunner of the National Association for the Advancement of Colored People, or NAACP. The NAACP still fights for equal rights for black people.

With Du Bois's support, the NAACP grew rapidly. By 1916, it had 9,000 members in 67 cities. Once, a police agent asked Du Bois what the NAACP was demanding for blacks. Du Bois replied, "the enforcement of the Constitution of the United States." He continued to work with the NAACP until 1934.

Du Bois standing at table ready to discuss his ideas for equal rights for African-Americans.

Until 1944, Du Bois was the chairman of the Department of Sociology at Atlanta University. While there, he wrote hundreds of essays and several books. But racism continued to frustrate Du Bois. After World War II, he became involved in socialism and the peace movement, which wanted to ban nuclear weapons.

Because of these involvements, Du Bois was put on trial at the age of 82. At his trial, he made this statement: "It is a sad commentary that we must enter a courtroom today to plead Not Guilty to something that cannot be a crime—advocating peace and friendship between the American people and the peoples of the world." Letters of support poured in from all over the world. The judge dropped the case.

Even though the charges were dropped, Du Bois's reputation was ruined. Publishers and magazines refused to publish his writings. Organizations would not hire him as a speaker. The FBI tapped his telephone and opened his mail. He was not allowed to travel outside the country.

When he was 93 years old, Du Bois joined the Communist Party. In 1963, he gave up his U.S. citizenship and moved to Ghana. He died there on August 27, 1963.

Although Du Bois had many troubles with the United States government, his influence is still felt. Because of his work with the NAACP, Du Bois helped give black people a voice.

Ida B. Wells-Barnett (1862–1931)

Civil Rights Leader

Between 1890 and 1900, over 1,200 American blacks were hung by mobs. Ida Wells-Barnett compiled a record of all these bloody lynchings. She called it "A Red Record." Thousands of people who read "A Red Record" joined together to try to end such crimes. Wells-Barnett's bravery helped to stop the lynching of blacks in America.

Ida Wells-Barnett

Ida Wells was born a slave in Mississippi. When she was 16, both of her parents died. Wells lied about her age to get a teaching job. She earned 25 dollars per month. This salary supported her and her five brothers and sisters. When Wells complained about the shabby conditions in the school, she was fired.

Wells began writing for *Free Speech*, a newspaper in Memphis, Tennessee. Because of her writing, the paper gained many more readers. In 1892, three black men were dragged from the Memphis jail and lynched. Ignoring death threats, Wells printed the names of the men who did the lynching, and the names of the city officials who allowed it to happen.

An African-American being dragged to his lynching.

She asked blacks not to use the Memphis streetcar line, and to leave town if possible. Within months, the streetcar line was almost bankrupt. Over 2,000 black people had moved away from Memphis.

During the early 1900s, lynching was considered an acceptable way to deal with black criminals. But the victims Wells wrote about were not even criminals. They had been jailed on phony charges because they were successful grocery store owners who were competing with a white-owned grocery store.

Wells thought that if the men in Memphis were innocent, other lynching victims might also have been innocent. She began traveling around the country, interviewing people who had witnessed lynchings. She investigated 728 lynchings, and found that about one-third of the victims had never been accused of a crime. Most had never had a trial. Many victims were murdered for "quarreling with whites" or "race prejudice."

Ida Wells continued to write angry editorials. She tried to shame police, judges, and mayors into stopping the lynchings. After one article, a mob burned her newspaper office in Memphis. Wells was out of town, but afterwards she decided to move to New York City. On June 5, 1892, the *New York Age* published an article by Wells. In it, she listed the names, dates, and details of hundreds of lynchings. The paper sold 10,000 copies.

In 1895, Wells married a lawyer named Ferdinand Lee Barnett. Together they organized black political groups and women's organizations. Wells-Barnett was one of the founders of the NAACP. Because of her brave efforts, people began to see lynching as a horrible crime.

Mary Church Terrell (1863–1954)

Advocate for Women's Rights

Mary Church Terrell was the daughter of a former slave named Robert Church. She went to Oberlin College in Ohio and received her masters degree in 1888. Her father thought that no man would want her if she studied higher mathematics. He disowned Mary because of this, but she continued to pursue her education. In 1895, Mary Church Terrell was appointed to the Board of Education in Washington, D.C. She was the first black woman in the country to hold such a position. But Terrell had difficulties with people who believed that women were inferior to men. She decided to fight back.

Terrell joined the women's groups who were fighting for the passage of the Nineteenth Amendment to the Constitution. The amendment would give women the right to vote. But the white women's groups did not want a black member. They were afraid it would hurt their position with southerners.

When World War I started, many black people moved north. They wanted to work in the factories when the white workers left to join the army. Because black women did not have protection from unions, Terrell began the Women Wage-Earners Association. This union organized black nurses, waitresses, and domestic workers. Terrell also helped to create the National Association of Colored Women and the NAACP.

At age 90, Terrell organized a boycott of Washington, D.C. department stores that refused to serve blacks. She also led a march on restaurants that refused blacks. Until the day she died, Mary Church Terrell fought for the rights of women and black people.

CHAPTER 3

BLACK INVENTORS

The turn of the last century was an age of invention. Motor cars, electric lights, cameras, and other inventions changed millions of people's lives. Before the Civil War, slaves were not allowed to hold patents, but free black men were. Blacks were responsible for many inventions that changed the world.

Jan Ernst Matzeliger (1852–1889)

Inventor

What Jan Matzeliger did for our feet was quite a feat. Matzeliger invented a machine that could stitch the bottoms on shoes in record time. He revolutionized the shoe industry around the world.

Matzeliger was born in Dutch Guiana (present-day Suriname) in South America. His mother was a black native of Guiana and his father was a wealthy Dutch engineer. Matzeliger went to work in a machine shop when he was 10-years-old. When he was 19, he worked aboard a ship. When the ship docked in Philadelphia, Pennsylvania, Matzeliger decided to stay in America.

In 1876, Matzeliger began to work for a shoe company in Lynn, Massachusetts. He also went to night school to learn physics. In his spare time he gave art lessons and painted.

Workers in a shoe factory in Lynn, Massachusetts, assemble shoes.

While working at the shoe factory, Matzeliger saw how long it took to stitch the bottom of a shoe to the top. Every shoe had to be stitched by hand. Workers could make only 40 pairs of shoes a day. Working at home at night, Matzeliger invented a machine that stitched shoes together. His first model was made from wood, wire, and cigar boxes. Matzeliger was offered 50 dollars for it, but he rejected the offer.

In 1880, Matzeliger invented a better version of his shoe-stitching machine. This one earned him an offer of 1,500 dollars, but again Matzeliger turned it down. In 1883, he received a patent from the U.S. Patent Office for his invention. It enabled a worker to produce up to 700 pairs of shoes a day.

With several other men, Matzeliger started the United Shoe Company. Within a few years, they were manufacturing 98 percent of the shoes made in the United States. Soon the company was worth 20 million dollars.

In 1886, Matzeliger became ill with tuberculosis. He died in 1889 and left all of his money to the North Congregational Church, the only church that had not rejected him because of his race. Sixty-five years after Matzeliger's death, the United Shoe Company was worth over one billion dollars. His technique for making shoes is still used all over the world.

Lewis Howard Latimer (1848–1928)

Draftsman, Inventor

When Alexander Graham Bell invented the telephone, his friend Lewis Latimer, a young black draftsman, drew up the plans for it. A draftsman is an artist who draws plans and inventions.

Latimer was born in 1848 in Boston, Massachusetts. His father deserted his family when he was 10-years-old, and Latimer had to go to work. When he was 18, he worked as an office boy for a company that patented inventions. The company employed several draftsmen. Latimer became fascinated with drafting. He purchased a set of used drafting tools. With the help of library books and other draftsmen, Latimer became an expert at drafting. Soon, he was the chief draftsman at the company where he had started as an office boy.

Alexander
Graham Bell
with telephone
invention.

During the course of his work, Latimer met Alexander Graham Bell. The two became good friends. Bell asked Latimer to make the drawings for the first telephone. Soon, Latimer began working on his own inventions.

In 1881, Latimer started working with electricity. He invented the Latimer Lamp, an improved light bulb that lasted longer and worked better than previous bulbs. Because of this, he was asked to help install electric light plants in New York City. He also worked with an electric company in England.

Thomas Edison in his laboratory.

In 1884, Latimer was asked to be a member of the Edison Pioneers, a small, exclusive group of scientists who worked with Thomas Edison. He continued to invent until his death in 1928.

George Washington Carver (1864–1943)

Scientist and Inventor

George Washington Carver might be the most famous black scientist ever. He invented one of America's favorite foods, peanut butter. In fact, Carver invented 325 products that could be made from peanuts. These included facial powder, coffee, ink, shampoo, vinegar, and soap.

George Carver was born in 1861. His parents were slaves. They lived on a plantation in Missouri that belonged to Moses and Susan Carver. When George was a baby, he and his mother were kidnapped by slave raiders and taken to Arkansas. Young George was returned to the Carver Plantation in Missouri, but his mother was never found.

George Washington Carver

Carver was sick as a child and could not work much. He spent his time wandering in the woods, collecting plants and flowers.

Carver taught himself to read. At age 10, he left the plantation to work at odd jobs and attend school. Carver was an excellent student when he attended high school in Kansas. He won a scholarship to Highland University, but the school refused to admit him when they found out he was black. Carver continued to work and save money. Several years later, he was accepted at Simpson College in Iowa. He supported himself by ironing clothes for his fellow students.

At Simpson, Carver decided to become a scientist. In 1891, he enrolled in the Iowa Agricultural College. His work in botany and chemistry earned him the respect of his teachers. Carver was asked to work at the college after graduation. He became an instructor and the director of the greenhouse. Soon, Carver was doing research on funguses that attack wheat, oats, and soybeans. In 1896, he received a letter from Booker T. Washington asking him to teach at Tuskegee Institute in Alabama.

Tuskegee was an all-black college started by Washington. It did not have much lab equipment, and it could not afford to pay Carver a good salary. But Carver decided to teach at Tuskegee anyway. He said, "It has always been the one great ideal of my life to be of the greatest good to the greatest number of people."

The soil in Alabama had been worn out from years of growing cotton. To solve this problem, Carver invented a system of crop rotation that used peanuts. Peanuts were planted in cotton fields. They improved the soil by replacing lost minerals. The program worked so well that soon there was a surplus of peanuts. Carver decided to find new uses for peanuts. Soon, farmers could earn more by farming peanuts than by farming cotton.

Carver also experimented with the sweet potato. He made 118 products from the sweet potato, including dyes and synthetic rubber. Because of his inventions, Carver became famous all over the world. He was visited by the crown prince of Sweden and the Prince of Wales. Henry Ford offered Carver $100,000 a year to work for

George Washington Carver at work.

Ford Motor Company. Thomas Edison made a similar offer. Carver turned them both down because he wanted to teach. He said, "Education is the key to unlocking the golden door of freedom."

Scientists today still value Carver's research. And anyone who likes to eat peanut butter and jelly sandwiches owes thanks to George Washington Carver.

Granville T. Woods (1856–1910)

Inventor

Granville T. Woods was known as the "Black Edison." In his lifetime he patented more than 60 inventions. His genius changed America's communication and transportation systems.

Woods was born in Columbus, Ohio, in 1856. He was forced to quit school and go to work when he was 10-years-old. Woods worked as a fireman and engineer on the railroads. At age 22, he studied electrical engineering on Ironsides, a British steamship.

In 1884, Woods started a machine shop in Cincinnati, Ohio. There he began making telegraph, electrical, and telephone equipment. Woods patented several devices by 1887, including a machine that could send messages to moving trains. His most important invention was the electrified "third rail" that powers subway systems. Though Woods died in 1910, his "third rail" is still used in subway systems all over the world.

A Subway in Brooklyn, New York, in the early 1900s.

CHAPTER 4

BLACKS IN WORLD WAR I

The United States entered World War I in 1917. Black men were drafted into the U.S. Army. Many of these men wondered if they would be treated fairly by the country they were called upon to defend. Oftentimes, the answer was no. Blacks served in segregated units. Many of these units had inferior equipment and hostile white commanders.

At first, blacks could not serve as officers. Then the Army announced that if 200 college-educated blacks signed up, they would be sent to a special officer-training school. Much to the Army's surprise, 1,500 men signed up. Fort Des Moines in Iowa trained about 600 black officers. Blacks, however, were not

African-American World War I sergeant

allowed in the Marines and were only allowed in the Navy as menial workers.

Black servicemen could not enter white theaters and restaurants. They were not allowed to use public transportation. Even the YMCAs on military bases did not allow blacks. These inequalities caused hundreds of fights and riots. In 1917, 39 blacks died in a race riot in St. Louis. Other riots occurred in Texas and South Carolina. The units involved were shipped to the worst war zones in Europe.

When black U.S. troops went to Europe, most were assigned to fight with French battalions. These French battalions were locked in deadly combat with the German Army. The United States instructed them not to treat the black soldiers as equals. But the battle-worn French Army ignored this advice. Many black soldiers

African-American troops in France. Part of the 15th Regiment Infantry, New York National Guard.

received the distinguished Croix de Guerre (Cross of War), France's highest military honor.

Black troops fought bravely for the United States. The Germans called the all-black 369th Infantry unit the "Hellfighters" because they never retreated and were never captured. Two men in the 369th, Sergeant Henry Johnson and Private Needham Roberts, fought off 30 German soldiers before finally being captured. Although seriously wounded, the two men managed to escape. Their bravery saved the lives of hundreds of other soldiers.

When World War I ended, President Woodrow Wilson said that "The world is safe for democracy." For many American blacks, however, true democracy and justice were still not a reality.

Nine African-American soldiers who won the Croix de Guere, return home.

TIMELINE

Late 1800s Sharecropping keeps many blacks in the South poor and over-worked

1890–1900 Over 1,200 blacks are hung by mobs

1892 The New York Age publishes an article by Ida Wells-Barnett listing the names, dates, and details of hundreds of lynchings; it sells over 10,000 copies

1895 Mary Church Terrell is appointed to the Board of Education in Washington, D.C.

1901 Last black congressman leaves office

1905 The Niagara Movement, forerunner of the NAACP, is formed by W.E.B. Du Bois

1916   NAACP grows to 9,000 members with branches in 67 cities

1917   United States enters World War I

———— Race riots break out in St. Louis, Texas, and South Carolina

1918   World War I ends

Early 1920's Harlem becomes the world's largest urban black community

1924   Alain Locke's *The New Negro* is published

1930   The Great Depression Begins

CHAPTER 5

THE HARLEM RENAISSANCE

By the end of World War I, the Harlem area of New York City had become the world's largest urban black community. Black people from Jamaica, Haiti, Cuba, Puerto Rico, and Africa mingled with American blacks from the North and South. The result was a lively mix of cultures and languages. The crowded streets of Harlem were alive with jazz, rumba, ragtime, spirituals, and even string quartets. Black artists, poets, musicians, authors, and actors flocked to Harlem. They all wanted to join the vigorous revival of the arts that came to be known as the Harlem Renaissance.

In 1924, Alain Locke published a book called *The New Negro.* It was a collection of poems, essays, stories, and pictures by black artists. *The New Negro* became very popular among New Yorkers of all races. White people began traveling to Harlem to visit art galleries and music clubs. After it caught on in New York, support for black culture spread to cities all over America. People began to see art as a way of easing racial tensions.

Harlem's dance crazes swept across the nation. Out of the Savoy Ballroom came the Charleston and the Lindy Hop. Playwrights and

Dancing the Lindy Hop at the Savoy Ballroom.

songwriters began using black themes. Plays such as *The Emperor Jones*, *Porgy and Bess*, and *Blackbirds* were produced on Broadway. Blues and jazz, the major styles of black American musicians, sold millions of records. As Alain Locke said, the 1920s were a "spiritual coming of age" for black culture in America. Here are some profiles of people who made America sit up and take notice during the Harlem Renaissance.

Damon Evans entertains his friends with a song about his attitude towards religion in a scene from the opera *Porgy and Bess*.

Langston Hughes (1902–1967)

Poet, Author

More black American authors and poets published books during the 1920s than in any previous decade. Most of these writers lived in Harlem. The premier poet of the Harlem literary movement was Langston Hughes. He wrote about black experiences in a stark, vivid style that few writers could match.

Langston Hughes was born in Joplin, Missouri, in 1902. His father left home shortly after he was born. Langston was raised by his grandmother, Mary. Mary's first husband had been an abolitionist who fought to end slavery. He was killed fighting alongside John Brown at his famous raid in Harpers Ferry, Virginia. All Mary had to remember her husband by was a bullet-riddled shawl that he had worn during the raid. When Langston was young, Mary would wrap herself in the shawl and tell him stories about Frederick Douglass, Harriet Tubman, and other famous abolitionists. When Langston slept, Mary would drape the shawl over him.

Langston Hughes

Langston began writing poetry at age 13. When he was 19, one of his poems was published in *The Crisis*, the most famous black magazine in the country. The poem, entitled "The Negro Speaks of Rivers," told of the black connection with the Nile, the Congo, and the Mississippi rivers. The last line reads, "My soul has grown deep like the rivers." The poem, which was first scribbled on the back of an envelope, is one of Hughes' most famous.

Hughes went to Columbia University in 1921, but he left college after one year and worked as a sailor on a freight ship. While he traveled to Africa and Europe, Hughes wrote dozens of poems . He lived in Paris, where he spent most of his time listening to black jazz musicians in the nightclubs.

Hughes moved to Washington, D.C., in 1924. There he worked as a busboy at the Wardman Park Hotel. Hughes showed his poems to Vachel Lindsay, a poet who was staying at the Wardman. Lindsay read Hughes's poems to an audience and the response was overwhelming. Soon Hughes was reading his poems to large crowds.

Hughes published a book of poetry in 1926 while enrolled at Lincoln University in Philadelphia. In 1930, he published his first novel, *Not Without Laughter*. It was an immediate success. For the next several years, Hughes traveled around the globe. In 1934, he published a book called *The Ways of White Folks*. In 1937, Hughes returned to Harlem and started the Suitcase Theater, where his plays packed the house night after night. Later, he founded theaters in Los Angeles and Chicago.

Over the years, Langston Hughes wrote plays, poems, novels, children's books, histories, biographies, and radio and television scripts. His books are still excellent reading for anyone interested in the hope, pain, humor, and anger that has surrounded the lives of black people in America.

William Christopher Handy (1873–1958)

Musician, Songwriter

Although W. C. Handy did not live in Harlem, his contributions paved the way for other black entertainers. Many of Harlem's best and brightest musicians were influenced by Handy. His name holds an honored place in black music history that few can match.

William Christopher Handy was born in Florence, Alabama. Because of his large ears, his mother predicted that he would be a musician. She was right. As a child, Handy made music with broom handles, combs, jugs, harmonicas, and anything else he could find. When he grew older, he traveled the country playing with small bands. Life on the road was not easy for a black man. Handy faced intolerance and discrimination everywhere he went. In many small towns, black men were not welcome after dark. That is why Handy wrote, "I hate to see that evening sun go down." During his career, he wrote many blues classics, including "St. Louis Blues," "Memphis Blues," and "Beale Street Blues."

When Handy traveled through the South, he secretly passed out

Composer W. C. Handy makes notations on sheet music while creating St. Louis Blues.

copies of a black newspaper called the *Chicago Defender*. This was a very dangerous thing to do. The paper urged southern blacks to move north, where there were better jobs and schools. Because white southerners did not want their supply of cheap, black labor to leave, they outlawed the *Defender* and lynched anyone who handed it out. Sheriffs even pulled black people off of trains that were headed north.

In 1918, Handy established the Handy and Pace Music Company. The company, which published jazz and blues songs, became an instant success. Before the 1920s, the blues were considered to be the music of poor, ignorant blacks. Thanks to W. C. Handy, this attitude changed. Although he went blind in 1943, he continued to write and publish the music of black Americans. Today, the blues are a respected musical form, in part because of the father of the blues, W. C. Handy.

Louis Armstrong

Louis Armstrong (1900–1971)

Musician

There were hundreds of "hot" musicians in Harlem in the 1920s. The swinging sound of jazz music was taking the country by storm. One of the hottest musicians in

Statue of Louis Armstrong in Armstrong Park in New Orleans, Louisiana.

Harlem was Louis "Satchmo" Armstrong, a trumpet player from New Orleans.

Louis Armstrong was born in 1900 on the Fourth of July. His family was very poor, and he was sent to live with his grandmother when he was five years old. Armstrong grew up in a section of New Orleans that was famous for its musicians and bands. When he was nine, he sang on street corners for pennies.

On New Year's Eve in 1913, Armstrong was arrested for shooting off a pistol at midnight. A judge sent him to the Colored Waif's Home for Boys. At the home, Armstrong learned to play the cornet. When he was released, he began playing jazz in local bands. To earn money, Armstrong also washed dishes, hauled coal, and collected junk. He played so well that Joe "King" Oliver, a famous musician, helped him perfect his technique.

By the time he was 18, Armstrong was playing music full time. After playing for a year on a Mississippi riverboat, he moved to Chicago where King Oliver's band was playing. Armstrong's incredible playing put him in the spotlight in King Oliver's band. By the end of their national tour, he was a famous musician.

In 1924, Armstrong moved to Harlem to join Fletcher Henderson's band. There he began to learn the trumpet, the instrument that he is best known for playing. Armstrong starred in the musical *Hot Chocolates*, which brought him even more fame. Later he played for England's King George during a tour of Europe.

Armstrong's rough singing voice earned him the nickname "Satchelmouth" or "Satchmo." By the time he died in 1971, Louie "Satchmo" Armstrong had toured the world several times and made over 50 movies. He rose from a life of poverty in New Orleans to become the King of Swing.

Edward Kennedy "Duke" Ellington (1899–1974)

Bandleader and Composer

Another shining star in Harlem's swinging jazz age was Duke Ellington. In his lifetime, he composed over 6,000 songs. He wrote scores for five movies and several musicals. His famous works have been played and recorded by thousands of musicians. Not bad for someone who had to be forced to practice the piano as a child.

Edward Kennedy Ellington was born in Washington, D.C. His friends nicknamed him "Duke" because he was always "duked out" in the finest clothes. Baseball and art were his favorite hobbies while growing up. He did not like having to practice the piano while his friends were outside playing ball. But when he finished high school, Ellington was offered a scholarship to Pratt Institute of Art in New York City. By then, he was dreaming of a career in music.

Duke worked at a soda fountain called the Poodle Dog Cafe. The cafe had a band, and sometimes he was asked to sit in. Inspired by the cafe, Duke wrote his first song. It was called "The Soda Fountain Rag." Before long, he was playing professionally.

Ellington took his band to New York City in 1922, where he met Fats Waller and other influential musicians. One year later, Ellington's band became a regular at the Hollywood Club at 49th and Broadway. In 1927, he began playing at Harlem's world-famous Cotton Club.

The Cotton Club hosted a weekly radio broadcast that was heard all over the country. Soon Ellington's theme song, "East St. Louis Toodle-Oo," was being broadcast nationwide. Ellington continued to play the Cotton Club for the next five years.

The 1930s were the time of the Depression. People could not afford to go to nightclubs, and Ellington's brand of swing music

Duke Ellington at the piano.

lost some of its popularity. Ellington, however, continued to compose. He kept his band together even while they were losing money. He said, "A musical profit is more important than a financial loss."

Ellington's fame continued to spread after World War II, and he continued to play throughout the world. By the time he died in 1974, Duke Ellington had become a legend in his own time. He brought the joy of swing to the lives of millions of people.

The night spot that best evokes glittering images of Harlem in the 1920s and 1930s is the Cotton Club (above). People could enjoy African-American entertainers like Louis Armstrong and Bill "Bojangles" Robinson at the elegant Cotton Club.

A Final Word

In the early 1900s, African-Americans were becoming more educated than ever before. Black people became scientists, inventors, musicians, politicians, actors, artists, and more. Although prejudice often slowed their progress, thousands of black men and women worked hard to change the world for the better.

The Harlem Renaissance of the 1920s was an especially great achievement for black culture. When the Depression hit in 1930, businesses closed down and 14 million Americans were out of work. African-Americans were often the first to be fired when hard times hit. Black schools lost funding, and black artists suffered. Nightclubs shut down and theaters closed their doors. A mood of despair fell across America. For many black people, the hard times got even harder.

But the outstanding works of Duke Ellington, Langston Hughes, and others gave hope to people who were struggling against poverty and prejudice. Their words, arts, and music shine today like they did in the 1920s. Society will remember their contributions for many years to come.

B y the end of World War I, the Harlem area of New York City had become the world's largest urban black community.

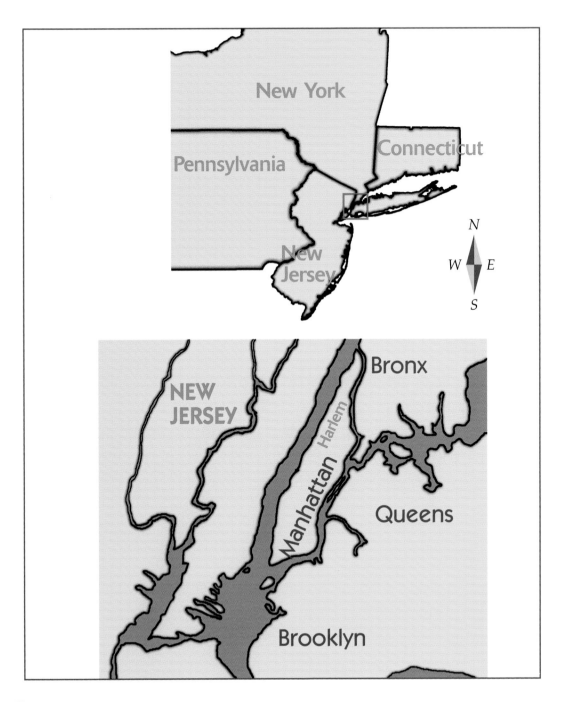

INTERNET SITES

The African-American Mosaic

http://lcweb.loc.gov/exhibits/african/afam001.html

> *This site details black history from the colonization of Liberia to Roosevelt's "new deal" in the 1930s. There are tons of links and pictures of important people and documents.*

African-American Odyssey—Library of Congress

http://lcweb2.loc.gov/ammem/aaohtml/

> *This Library of Congress site contains a history of blacks in America from slavery to civil rights with pictures, links to other sites, and a collection of works by influential blacks in history.*

Harlem Renaissance

www.nku.edu/~diesmanj/harlem.html

> *A web site about the Harlem Renaissance with history, poetry, artwork of the period, and links to other historical sites.*

GLOSSARY

Botany—The science of plant life.

Chain Gang—A group of prisoners chained together that the state rented out to private industry for hard labor. Even the smallest of crimes earned a black man a spot on the chain gang digging ditches, building roads, or farming crops for no pay. Black and white striped clothes made chain gangs very recognizable.

Convict Lease System—Policy whereby blacks who committed crimes were given sentences on a chain gang and rented out to private industries for hard labor. The state made a lot of money with this system.

Croix de Guere—The highest honor awarded by the French military. Most black American soldiers in World War I were sent to fight with the French who were in heavy combat with the Germans. Many black soldiers were awarded the Croix de Guere (Cross of War) by the French military for their fierce fighting.

Draftsman—An artist who draws plans and sketches, usually for machinery or structures.

Exploitation—an unjust use of another person for one's own profit.

Harlem Renaissance—During the 1920s, blacks from the Caribbean, Africa, and America gathered in Harlem, at the time the world's largest urban black community. There they spawned a new age of the arts deriving from black culture. Black music, literature, and theater rose to prominence and brought black culture to America's attention.

Ku Klux Klan—A secret organization founded in the southern United States after the Civil War that advocated white rule by intimidating and violently attacking blacks.

Lynching—The hanging or killing of someone by a mob as punishment for a presumed crime or offense. Many blacks were chased-down, beaten, and hung by groups like the Ku Klux Klan, often for no other reason than the color of their skin.

NAACP—The National Association for the Advancement of Colored People was a group that grew out of W.E.B. Du Bois' Niagara Movement. The group sought equal rights for blacks and "the enforcement of the Constitution of the United States." The organization still exists today.

Niagara Movement, The—A group of black leaders and educators organized by W.E.B. Du Bois to help fight for the rights of blacks. This group was the forerunner of the NAACP.

Patent—An exclusive right granted by the Government to an inventor for the product or process invented. A patent holder is the only one that can manufacture, use, or sell the patented invention. Patents last for 17 years and the holder can sell the patent rights at any time.

Sharecropping—The process whereby free blacks who could not afford land or supplies to farm would work for their previous owners for a share of their crop's profits and a one-room cabin to live in. The land owners often overcharged the blacks, keeping them from making much money. This practice made being a sharecropper not much better than being a slave.

INDEX